W9-BYA-301

THE RAQQA DIARIES:
ESCAPE FROM "ISLAMIC STATE"

THE RAQQA DIARIES: ESCAPE FROM "ISLAMIC STATE"

BY SAMER*

EDITED BY MIKE THOMSON

Illustrations by Scott Coello
Translation by Nader Ibrahim
Co-edited by John Neal

Interlink Books

An imprint of Interlink Publishing Group, Inc.
Northampton, Massachusetts

الطغاة يجلبون الغزاة

ابن خلدون

The tyrants bring the invaders

Ibn Khaldun, 14th century Arab historian

In areas of Syria and Iraq controlled by so-called Islamic State (IS),[1] the penalty for speaking to the Western media is death by beheading. That fact highlights not only the courage but also the conviction of anti-IS activists like our brave diarist.

When Samer (not his real name) began writing these diaries, he lived in Raqqa, the capital of IS's self-proclaimed caliphate in eastern Syria and one of the most isolated cities on earth. Internet cafés there are monitored closely by IS, and mobile phone lines can often be traced. It is almost impossible for foreign journalists like me to get in, and locals are forbidden to leave without permission. Some of those caught trying to do so have been executed. But after several months of nervy and often interrupted conversations, we finally managed to make contact with a small activist group in Raqqa called Al-Sharqiya 24. Trust slowly grew between us, and finally one of their members courageously agreed to write a personal diary of his recent experiences there. What followed is an extraordinary and chilling insight into how the brutality and injustices perpetrated by IS permeates almost every level of life in its now infamous capital.

To help protect Samer, his words were encrypted and sent to a third country before being passed on to the BBC. Names and other details have been changed for the same reason.

Getting the diaries out of Raqqa was often a heart-stopping experience. Sometimes, for days on end, calls to our author and his group would go unanswered. My colleagues and I were often left wondering whether they had all been caught by IS. It was a horrible feeling. On one occasion we heard news that two anti-IS activists who had managed to get over the border into Turkey

1 Also referred to in this book as Daesh.

had been beheaded. We feared at first that one of them might be Samer. Fortunately, we finally managed to contact him the following day.

Much of the media coverage of Syria has, inevitably, looked more at the political and military side of the conflict than the way it has effected people's everyday lives. This makes it harder for those living far away from it all to truly understand the suffering it is causing civilians there. It also makes it more difficult for us to relate to the individuals we hear about, even though they share the same hopes, needs, dreams and fears as ourselves. The personal accounts of our diarist bridge that gap in an extraordinary way.

I have wondered what makes somebody speak out in the way Samer has, knowing that by doing so he is putting at risk not only himself, but also those he holds dear. The answer becomes clear in his diaries. Having seen friends and relatives butchered, his community's life shattered and the local economy ruined by notorious extremists, our courageous diarist believes he is fighting back by telling the world what is happening to his beloved city.

Samer's brave words have affected me deeply. Despite the fact that we are separated by thousands of miles, it feels like his family have become my family, his friends my friends, his frightening world mine too.

Mike Thomson
BBC Foreign Affairs Correspondent
August 2016

Media activists are the thorn in the side of Syria's current tyrants. The Assad regime, which has tyrannised Syrians for the last forty years, has allowed the invaders, Daesh, to impose an equally perverse reign of terror on the Syrian people. It is no surprise then that the regime has imprisoned and tortured thousands of media activists, and that Daesh dedicates time and manpower to hunting them down and devising extreme ways to kill them.

While the regime besieges towns and cities physically, Daesh besieges communities by cutting off their communication to the outside world. Limited mobile phone coverage, monitoring at internet cafés, no 3G, alleged listening-in to landline calls, no access to newspapers, and now Daesh has begun destroying satellite dishes. It does not want others' stories to be known. As a result, it dominates the media landscape inside and outside. It is only brave activists who undermine Daesh's monopoly by risking their lives to report the truth to the outside world. But they are few. Were the communications siege to be broken, people living inside Daesh territory would have access to the outside world, and vice versa. Their online presence would provide journalists with an alternative narrative, dilute the effectiveness of Daesh propaganda and expose its lies.

We dedicate this book to Syria's media activists. In memory of those, our friends, who have been killed for daring to expose tyranny. May Allah protect you. And for those of us who continue this courageous work, may we continue to be safe and successful. Only through perseverance will we achieve the revolution's goals, which we used to chant in the streets in 2011: 'Freedom, dignity, justice.'

Al-Sharqiya 24
August 2016

I'm one of many who continue to suffer at the hands of the Syrian regime, and its offspring, Daesh.

Samer

6th March 2013

One morning, everyone in the city woke up to the sound of explosions and gunfire. My God, I thought, what is happening? Has revolution against the government finally arrived?

Then came some frantic banging and shouting outside our house. When my father opened the door, our neighbour grabbed hold of his arm and screamed at the top of his voice: 'They've done it! They've done it! The rebels have entered our city…they've taken over!'

My father asked if he was joking. But our neighbour insisted that the police and army were gone; some had been killed but the rest had just run away. They were no longer in the city.

I couldn't believe what I was hearing. I ran outside and saw cars flying the flag of the Free Syrian Army. One of the cars stopped right in front of me. A man leaned out of the window and told me not to be afraid. He said he and his fellow soldiers had come to liberate us all from tyranny and corruption. 'We are your brothers,' he added.

I asked him if I would still be able to go back to university to finish my education. He replied that yes, everything would be OK once they'd got rid of the tyrants. My head was spinning, I couldn't believe all this was happening.

Within a few hours, everything became clearer. The Free Syrian Army, Ahrar al-Sham and the Al-Nusra Front had taken control of our city.

In the evening, still very excited, I met up with my friends. We sat and discussed what to do now. We all agreed that we should give our full support to the Free Syrian Army since they were all Syrians like us and shared our goals. We all wanted to be freed from Assad's regime. But we didn't know quite what to make of the two Islamist groups – Daesh and the Al-Nusra Front – who had helped liberate our city. We were a bit worried about them.

I will never forget the time when Daesh first appeared on the streets of our city. At first opposition forces surrounded the fighters who occupied the government buildings. We were optimistic. But then everything changed. The Free Syrian Army began to weaken. It was busy fighting the regime elsewhere and its forces around Raqqa became thinner and thinner. Its soldiers were hit by repeated government air strikes. Daesh fought back, broke the FSA's siege and quickly took over our helpless city.

They took advantage of our confusion and ignorance and began persuading people to join their ranks. At first they would charm people with a softly spoken manner, promising them the world. But I didn't buy any of this.

Daesh members come in two basic types. Those who actually believe they have come to save us were amongst the first to enter the city; the second type are much more violent.

The first time I saw the Hisba, Daesh's religious police, patrolling the streets, they were shouting at a woman who was pulling her daughter back onto the pavement after the little girl had run into the road. The mother looked very decent, according to local standards anyway. She was wearing an abaya[2] and a hijab,[3] but they were calling her really bad names and questioning her honour because she wasn't wearing a face veil. They were using words that most of us would be too ashamed to say. How could they call themselves religious? I wondered.

The young woman was becoming increasingly frightened and was trying to get away from them. She said she just wanted to take her daughter home, but they wouldn't leave her alone. By this time there were a few of us standing nearby; we were all shocked but didn't risk saying anything. It was then that Abo-Saeed decided to intervene. Since he'd retired about a decade ago, he'd been the muezzin[4] at the nearby mosque. Around the city, people were used to hearing his voice coming over the loudspeakers. If we didn't hear him calling people to prayer at night, we'd wonder what had happened. Now he started shouting back, demanding to know whether this was the holy message they were trying to spread. 'I swear,' he said, 'you have nothing to do with Islam.' He was popular and people began to gather around him. It made us feel braver to stand behind our local muezzin as he laid into these strangers who had appeared in our city out of nowhere. In the end, Abo-Saeed got so worked up he suffered a heart attack, right there in the street. While a few onlookers carried him to a nearby car and rushed him to hospital, we all began pushing forward. Soon an angry mob was surrounding the Daesh patrol. Evidently scared of what might happen next, the men wriggled free and ran away.

2 Loose-fitting full-length robe.
3 Traditional covering for the hair and neck.
4 The person appointed to lead and recite the call to prayer at the mosque.

'What brought them here?' I heard somebody ask. We all agreed that we didn't want them. A man in front of me called on everyone to stop saying such things. He warned that Daesh had got spies everywhere now. 'Didn't you hear what happened last night?' he said. 'They beheaded a guy in Naeem Square because he was saying bad things about them.' Ignoring that warning, a soulful voice behind me shouted, 'These people will take us back to the Dark Ages.'

I wonder what Daesh will do next. First they take over our city, then they tell people how to dress before setting up religious police and enforcing Sharia law. What on earth will they think of tomorrow?

Daesh has started taking revenge on everyone who opposes them: hunting down revolutionaries as well as other activist figures and those who support them. They accuse them of apostasy, but it's just another excuse for an execution. Every day they make a crowd gather in the square, as if they are about to stage a play. They also carry out some of these brutal punishments on roundabouts right in the middle of busy roads. They are determined that as many people as possible will witness what happens to those who displease them.

I can't believe what is happening. With each passing day the arrogance of Daesh increases and its evil grip on the city tightens. There is currently no way to challenge its control. It has taken many weapons from Assad's defeated soldiers, some of whom are regularly paraded and killed. Daesh arrests them and then gathers them together in large numbers. Its men line them up and execute them. The aim is to instil so much fear into the hearts of onlookers that nobody will dare to challenge their reign of terror.

Things here are getting worse and worse, darker and darker. It is the worst period anyone in Raqqa has witnessed. Optimism has died.

I hear loudspeakers saying that some people are about to be executed. A group of blindfolded men stand in handcuffs. In front of them a masked man begins reading out the sentences.

Hassan has been fighting with the regime forces. His punishment is beheading.

Eissa, a media activist, is accused of speaking to foreign parties. His punishment: beheading.

A man with a sword carries out the executions.

We are unable to do anything about what is happening in front of us. It's very dangerous to let your true feelings show because Daesh is eyeing the crowd; we are utterly in their grip. I stare into the faces around me, trying to read the thoughts behind the many sad, quiet eyes. In some I see anger. These angry faces stare at the executioner, doubtless plotting the revenge they will take against him when the opportunity comes. Many here are waiting for the spark that will ignite the uprising against that man and all Daesh murderers.

People are holding back for now out of fear, but surely not for much longer. While I am lost in thought, some people behind me start peeling away, desperate to leave this awful scene without being noticed. But this is very risky. Daesh is determined to ensure that we all watch the killings before us.

I heard the name of one of my neighbours being called out over the speakers. Somehow I couldn't stop myself going over. His decapitated head was on the ground. I couldn't stand up; my legs just wouldn't hold me. I can't get this image out of my mind.

As I walked down the road, cursing out loud, a group of IS religious police rushed over and grabbed me. They took me to their headquarters. I tried to reason with them, but it was no use. 'You were cursing out loud. Your punishment is forty lashes.'

Without any mercy or humanity, a man lashed me. I could see in his eyes that he took pride in this.

When I arrived at my front door, I collapsed. After hearing what had happened to me, my pregnant sister went into shock and began bleeding heavily. We knew we had to get her to a gynaecologist as quickly as possible, but when we arrived at the clinic, we found it was shut. A man outside told me that the doctor, who had been his neighbour for years, had been arrested by IS and they had shut down his clinic. Male doctors were now forbidden to treat female patients.

While some of Daesh's members are busy executing people for nothing, others spend their time creating friction. They provoke people in order to get a reaction. Then they punish anyone who opposes or criticises them. Every time Daesh move into a new chapter in their book of horrors, they change the leaders charged with inflicting whatever barbaric oppression they have in mind.

On the way home, I met my friend Abu-Muhammed, who runs a shop. He pointed to a store across the road owned by a man we'd known for many years. A group of IS men were speaking to him. One of them was holding a bunch of papers in his hands. As we crossed the road towards them, they moved on to the store next door.

'Hey!' one of them shouted to us. 'Who owns this shop?'

Abu-Muhammed replied that it was his.

'We're from Zakah,' the man told us. This is supposed to be a charity for the poor but acts as a kind of tax collector for IS. 'We're here for the money you owe us.'

Abu-Muhammed insisted that he'd already paid all that was due.

'Shut up!' the IS man bellowed back. 'You must pay us a hundred thousand Syrian pounds.'

Abu-Muhammed gasped that that was too much money. But he agreed to pay as soon as he could.

The severed heads of others who have crossed IS are hung on park fences and lamp posts. They act as a brutal warning.

That night our home was rocked by explosions. I saw bombers high above. I switched on the TV to hear the news that the international coalition was launching its first air strikes against IS.

The next day, there were an unusual number of Daesh members on the streets. A local cab driver warned me to be careful. He told me that coalition planes had hit many of Daesh's buildings last night. They had suffered lots of casualties and were out looking for civilians who might have guided the planes to their targets.

The cabbie was about to drive off when a man shouted, 'Stop! Stop!' He was a member of the new traffic police. They're all over the city now. He bellowed at the driver, demanding that he show him his licence and insurance papers. The cab driver showed him his licence, but didn't have any insurance. It has been more than two years since local motorists here have been able to get that.

'No insurance! Pay the penalty fine now,' the traffic policeman said, 'or I will impound your car.'

The driver was made to hand over five thousand Syrian pounds. This was more, he told me, than he earned in a whole week. 'They're not interested in traffic,' he mumbled. 'All they care about is fleecing us.'

A crowd had gathered around a deep hole. Crouched inside it was a woman. I asked people who she was and what she was doing there.

Before I got an answer, a large masked man declared: 'This woman was adulterous and her punishment is to be stoned to death.'

His words were interrupted by the noise of planes overhead. A street vendor shouted, 'Hide! Hide!'

The marketplace was hit. There were huge explosions, and body parts everywhere. It was a Russian air strike supposedly targeting terrorists.

Isn't the terrorism we suffer on the ground enough? Now you bring it from the skies as well.

There are massacres every day now all over Syria. Death comes from bombings, rocket attacks and all sorts of other weapons too. The constant drone of planes above us destroys all our happier moods. Everything is bloody and dying, except the regime. It feeds on darkness and grows ever stronger. Most of Raqqa's residents cannot understand what has happened. It overwhelms us. It's too much for any sane person to take in.

My brothers, sisters and I had planned a small party for Mother's Day. It was a cold March morning and I heard the sound of warplanes. I immediately set out for home.

As the taxi got closer, clouds of smoke filled the air.

The regime's planes had hit our street. Our neighbour's roof had collapsed onto ours. There were ambulances everywhere, and people running around carrying the dead and the injured.

One of my neighbours told me that my parents were hurt and had been taken to the general hospital. The feeling I had was indescribable. Judging by the way our house looked, I was expecting the worst. The top floor was completely destroyed and much of the ground floor was badly damaged too. Our neighbour's house was in a similar state.

When my brothers, sisters and I arrived at the hospital, the smell of blood and death filled the place. We were asked to look at the bodies laid out in front of us to see if our parents were amongst them.

I was in such a state of shock at that moment that I suddenly couldn't remember anything. As I stood beside my father, it was like nothing that had happened before that moment mattered. There was my dad. His body was littered with injuries. They had covered most of his corpse with a white sheet, but his face was still showing. I could see blood seeping through the sheet from numerous cuts. The telltale sign of shrapnel wounds.

I was overwhelmed with a sense of absolute loneliness and collapsed on the floor. I had lost my mentor, my guide in life, the man who always had an answer to everything. This was one of the darkest moments of my life. My father's death has continued to haunt me. It's changed something in me.

'Your mother is being treated in here,' a voice said quietly, 'but don't go in yet.'

Two hours passed and finally a doctor came out. I told him that I was her son. 'I've managed to save her life, but she's very sick,' he said.

After my father's funeral my family's dear, generous friend, Abu Muhammed, joined with our neighbours in helping to repair our bomb-damaged home. One gave us some cement and another provided metal rods, which enabled us to put two rooms back together again and repair the courtyard outside. Some parts of the house were so badly damaged that they are impossible to put right, but we managed to make most of the rest of it habitable again.

My mother's health has been deteriorating and she has been feeling very frail and vulnerable while we've been staying with friends. She was so relieved to be able to move back home.

Our life in Syria, with all its simplicity and innocent dreams, is a product of how our parents and their families were raised. We were brought up the same way as them, and we follow the path that they did. Everybody dreams that things will get better, a future full of the beauty of life and all it has to offer. But in our country, which lags behind many others in science and technology, such hopes often end in disappointment.

Not much happened during the period between the end of my childhood and the start of my life as a young man. It wasn't a very exciting time. I continued with my studies, and finished high school with really good grades. I then went on to university. Although I was enjoying my time there, things were happening around me that didn't encourage me to finish my course. After graduating, my older brother struggled to prosper from all his hard work. First he had to do military service, and then he worked without a proper contract for seven years in a government job. My cousin, who was also a university graduate, never got a job he wanted. He ended up painting walls for a living.

It was during my first-year studies that I fell in love for the first time. It started out as simple eye contact, but soon developed into so much more. The experience unleashed many emotions deep inside me. This girl and I had a beautiful time together. We shared our thoughts, our dreams and our ambitions. We planned a future together as man and wife. Our relationship continued for quite some time. It inspired and motivated me and gave me new hope in life.

I always spoke to her about how I wanted to travel abroad to continue my studies. But she would tell me off, insisting that I should stay in my country. I tried to convince her to come with me, saying we should travel together and escape the bitter reality around us. It was another dream that never came true, just like my dream of studying architecture.

I remember so clearly when we first met. It was in a lecture hall. It was one of the few times we both studied in the same place. I would often skip my own lectures and go to hers instead, just to see her. I tried to be useful, too. I would take notes in her lecture in case she needed help with her studies later. Then there were all those memorable morning coffees that we shared in the university café, side by side. I adored her. I still feel happy every time I picture her smiling. Memories of that smile mean the world to me. Sometimes when I think of it, even when I am out in the street, a beaming grin spreads across my face. People must think I'm crazy. But it's all down to sweet memories of her.

We had decided to commit to each other, but back then we had no idea what was about to hit us.

Her brother was arrested by Daesh. They accused him of working with the Free Syrian Army and threatened to execute him. But then they sent one of their men to 'negotiate' with her family. Daesh made them an offer. They would set her brother free on one condition. She must marry one of their fighters.

She called me to tell me the news. The tone of her voice said it all. I knew I was about to hear something terrible. Her words pierced my heart like the shrapnel that killed my father and destroyed our home. I was in pieces. But I knew that her brother's life was more important than our feelings and the dreams we shared. A life is worth much more than those things, or so I told myself repeatedly. I still try to convince myself of this.

I try not to question the many terrible things that have happened to me, or think too much about them. I look at others around me. Some have been even less fortunate, their positions much worse than mine.

I know that if I am to keep going and stay alive, I must not dwell on the sadness in my heart. I have to stay away from all of that. I have to keep busy. So I do. I take on things that cause me trouble but keep me occupied both physically and mentally. It seems my journey is far from over.

How I miss that love of mine. The woman I shared all my troubles with. Now I must deal with everything myself.

✳

As one of the older sons, I was expected to look after my younger siblings. My mother often helped me whenever this responsibility became too much. She always backed up whatever advice I'd already given my little brothers and sisters. If I hadn't been able to come up with a solution to their problems, she referred the matter to my father. He always seemed to have an answer. This kept a calm and loving atmosphere in our house. We all had a lot of respect for each other and any rows I had with my parents never lasted long. In fact, looking back, I think these often did me good and actually helped make us closer.

My dad used to tell us off when we didn't do our homework properly, or when we didn't study hard enough. He was very keen on education, and always encouraged us to go further, but I used to wonder why. When I looked around me, most of our friends, our cousins, our neighbours, scraped a living in poorly paid trades or worked for themselves. Even my father had to hold down two jobs.

My dad only ever bought us one present. It was originally for my brother but each of us passed it on to our younger siblings as we grew older. I still remember that present clearly. So much so that it's like I was playing with it yesterday. That little toy made me and my brothers and sisters so happy. It was a train with five carriages. My father would point at the first carriage and tell me: 'Samer, this carriage is yours. You're the driver of this train.' I've never forgotten that. Even though it was just a toy, it was very symbolic. My oldest brother had left home and it was clearly my dad's way of telling me that I had a responsibility towards my younger siblings. 'No one lives forever,' he would say. Now I understand what he meant by that.

Despite working at two jobs, my father couldn't normally afford to buy us presents because there were so many other things we needed. Like clothes, books, stationery and school fees, even though school was meant to be free. We knew how hard he worked and appreciated everything he did for us. We used to make up excuses to stay up late to see him when he came home. We missed him so much.

I remember one awful time when my father didn't come home. Throughout the night my mum kept coming into my room. The next morning she got us all up earlier than usual. She asked us to call in at my father's workplace on our way to school to see if his colleagues might know why he hadn't come home.

But when we got there, we were shocked to find that he hadn't turned up for his evening shift the night before and his boss had assumed that he was ill. My brother and I decided to skip school and spend the day looking for him.

We kept thinking of all the love and respect we had for him. His encouraging words about our studies echoed in our heads and we became increasingly terrified about what might have happened to him. But every time we went somewhere to ask if people had seen him, the answer was always no. We went everywhere we could think of, checking police stations, clinics, hospitals and all his friends' houses. We couldn't find a trace of him anywhere. We had only one place left to look. It was a building in the centre of town where he worked during the day.

There was definitely something fishy going on. Everywhere we went in this building, people claimed they hadn't seen him. In many cases they insisted they didn't know him at all, even though their faces said otherwise. How could people who had worked alongside him for so long suddenly not remember him? Something bad must have happened.

Me and my brother left, thinking we must have gone to the wrong building. Maybe we had made a mistake and our father worked somewhere else. In the end we decided to go back home and tell our mother what we'd discovered.

Her face was indescribable. She tried to hide her despair by telling us off for not going to school that day. She told us that our father was travelling for a while, and that must be why he was not around. Then she tried to comfort us, saying that we shouldn't worry. But he had simply disappeared. It was as if he had passed away.

Even though we were used to not seeing our father around very much, we missed him a lot. And we missed him more and more each day. Anyone who travels is supposed to come back, aren't they? we would say to each other.

With all these worries and unanswered questions flooding my head, and my fears and doubts growing by the minute, I decided to eavesdrop on a conversation my mother was having one day with my aunt and uncle. Apparently my father's manager had reported him as a dissident, saying he had been critical of the Assad family and their policies. It seems it was this claim that led to him being detained by the authorities. But nobody knew where he was being held.

The days all seem the same now. The revolution sparked my hopes and dreams. I dreamt of leaving my country and building a better life elsewhere, but that's no longer possible.

I remember how optimistic I was at the start of the revolution. My discontent with the ruling regime had been bottled up since I was young. I saw the evidence of the government's failed policies right in front of me and I couldn't do anything about it.

I remember how I went to Damascus with my mother to meet a man who said he'd be able to help release my father. Even though this man was a relative, my mother was told that she wouldn't be getting a discount on his usual charges. He was to mediate between my mother and the government official who was handling my father's case. She hoped he might be able to fast-track my dad's release before he was transferred to the 'investigations department'. If he was transferred there, it would be too late for such intervention and he might disappear for ever. We all feared that he might suffer the same fate as a relative of my uncle, who spent many years in jail.

It was my first time visiting the capital city. Although Damascus was much bigger than our city, it was similar to it in many ways. It still had inner-city neighbourhoods that

resembled ours, in their simplicity and friendly people. The only difference was the size of the streets. In Damascus they were much bigger. There were also more parks. Our city only had two parks, and one of these had a graveyard in it. We were too scared to go there alone.

I did not know this relative of my mother's that she had come to seek help from, though I had seen his picture around. When we arrived at his house in the evening, he was out with a friend who was a government official. His wife welcomed us, and showed us into a room where we could rest after our long journey. I wasn't tired. I just wanted to play with the relative's children and get to know them. But they all looked at me in a very condescending way. Their accent was different from ours, even though their parents came from the same place as us. They'd been born and raised in the capital and saw it as their home. I was really bothered by how they looked down at my town and everyone who lived there.

The children's behaviour started to make more sense when I overheard their mother talking. She was telling my mother about how difficult life used to be for her in the area where we still lived. She was describing it in a way I didn't like. She was calling people there stupid, saying that all they did was work on farms and look after cattle. She was talking about the place with disgust, even though all the vegetables she ate and the milk her children drank came from that area.

The next morning we went to the relative's office. It was full of people. They were all here to get their requests and deals looked at or officially approved. His office was like that of a minister of public affairs. We had to stand in a queue, even though we'd told the receptionist that we were related to him.

After a few minutes, a woman in the queue began speaking to the secretary. She'd overheard my mother say that we were related to the mediator. The woman told the secretary that she too was related to the mediator, even though this was a lie. She obviously hoped it would mean she would get to see him quicker. The woman was there because she needed help with her case. She couldn't afford to pay the council fees required to build on a piece of land she had just inherited.

Finally it was our turn and we entered the mediator's office. I was expecting some sort of warm welcome, but he spoke to us as if we were just another group of people looking for help.

After hearing our case, he initially refused to help on the grounds that it was political. Instead of praising my father for his brave moral stand, he said he only had himself to blame, adding that he shouldn't have got involved in 'managerial matters'. No one should ever criticise a government official for stealing from his country, he said. After all, he continued, such a person might need to use public money to build a palace for himself to 'make the country look more civilised'. Or maybe he would go on to be really successful in business and become one of the country's top businessmen and wealth creators. And that was why officials should be allowed to do what they wanted.

He insisted that we shouldn't try to get help from government officials about something my father had no right to complain about. What we needed to do was to appeal to the 'generosity' and 'kindness' of my father's boss, and seek his forgiveness for the terrible thing my father had done. That 'terrible thing' was my father complaining about the awful situation in the country and how difficult it was for him to make enough money to look after his family.

I was utterly disgusted by what this man, a relative of ours, was saying. But I learnt a valuable lesson about the

connection between oppression and corruption. It's like Abd al-Raman al-Kawakibi[5] once said: 'Oppression is the root of all corruption.'

Winning over my father's boss proved costly, but it worked. To pay for the deal, my mother had to sell all her jewellery, as well as a small piece of land that my father had inherited from his grandfather. After all he had achieved over the years, my father was back at square one, without a job. In the end, he was able to persuade his old boss to reduce his punishment and give him back his position. But this was in Raqqa itself, which meant he would have to leave very early in the morning and be back so late that he could no longer work a second job. And the cost of commuting was very high. In the end, it was decided that he would have to sell the share he had kept in our home and that we should all move to the city. I couldn't understand how someone could take everything we knew from us like this. Not only was all this happening under the eyes of the government, it had their complete support.

But I felt like change was coming and that there would be a solution to the suffering of our people. After all, things had got so bad that change seemed inevitable. The feeling kept getting stronger, and in my third year at university, the spark of revolution ignited the south. I felt a calling to serve the land that I had been raised to love and cherish. The needs of our country felt more important than our own individual welfare. We didn't believe that the international community would stand with its hands behind its back, watching

---

5   A nineteenth-century Syrian writer.

crimes being committed against unarmed people who were demanding rights that they were entitled to.

The Hama massacre of 1982 taught our people a valuable lesson. Under the command of the country's president, Hafez al-Assad,[6] the regime ended up killing more than 35,000 civilians in the heart of Syria, yet there were no repercussions. No journalists covered the atrocities, so people didn't know they had happened.

We remember this. That's why we make sure that anything that happens in this war is documented and published online through social media outlets. When the protests started at my university, I filmed them. I carried on when they spread to my neighbourhood and the rest of the city.

Having witnessed the ruthlessness of the regime in the past, our elders warned us to keep our protests peaceful. They told us that the regime didn't care what the UN Security Council said because it was protected by certain world powers and had political bargaining chips it could use. All of this became clear as time went by.

Even though the international community could clearly see what was going on, it didn't act. Crimes were being committed against Syrian people from every part of society. The regime tried to play the sectarian card and pit Sunnis against Shias, but this failed. The Syrian people refused to be manipulated like this.

The regime would try and convince its soldiers and police that the protestors they were suppressing were out to cause chaos and ruin the country. But the truth was as bright as the sun; everyone could see it. And it was clear that the people weren't going to give up until their demands were met.

6 Father of the current president.

I strongly believe that if the most basic of those demands had been met at the start, we wouldn't be where we are now, because the whole regime would have collapsed. We called for a lifting of the state of emergency, which would have put an end to the security forces clamping down and arbitrarily arresting us.

Our numbers grew as we kept on protesting. The bare chests of the protestors were up against the regime's full war machine. Demonstrations at the university were met with live bullets from security forces. More and more people were arrested. They would disappear for long periods of time, locked up in prisons or detention centres without any record that they were there. Some were executed. We were protesting on a daily basis, demanding the release of our friends. Then my turn came. Security forces attacked our demonstration and arrested dozens of us, including me.

We were taken first to one of their holding centres. Then I was sent to the Political Security Directorate, where the beatings and torture began. They tried to get me to confess to being a member of a terrorist organisation controlled by a Western party. When I refused to confess, they beat me even harder and the torture got worse. When my health deteriorated, they finally released me, but not before I was made to sign some papers pledging to take no further part in any protests. One of the papers I signed was blank. I have no idea what further things I am supposed to have admitted or agreed to.

This didn't stop me. If anything, it made me more rebellious. During one of the big protests in a public square involving thousands of people furious about the ongoing repression and murders, I saw one of the men who had tortured me. There he was, among us, in the heart of the protestors. He looked over and recognised me.

I told everyone who he was, that he was filming us all for the Political Security Directorate. He heard me and threatened to come to my university and arrest me again. He said his colleagues would make sure that I disappeared. There were checkpoints all over the city and I knew that my name would be on the regime's list.

That was the end of my education. I went into hiding.

At the start of the revolution, the safest places for people like me were areas with high concentrations of other anti-regime rebels. Security patrols who would arbitrarily arrest anyone who spoke out didn't dare enter the inner parts of neighbourhoods like these.

I took shelter in one such place, Joura, a district of Deir Ezzor, a city north of Damascus. It was one of the first revolutionary neighbourhoods and soon became home to many activists and defectors. It's an inner-city neighbourhood but provides shelter for people from rural areas too. Although very poor, people there were generous and kind to me. It reminded me of my childhood in my home town, before my family moved to Raqqa.

The Joura neighbourhood suffered a lot after the regime unleashed part of the presidential guard on it. They are considered to be some of Assad's most brutal and criminal units. To this day, the area continues to suffer from a double siege at the hands of both the regime and Daesh.

I only stayed there for around two months. After that I moved to another neighbourhood where civilians had begun carrying arms. They got together with defectors from the regime and formed an armed faction to protect the area. These people bravely repelled attempts by the regime's forces to get into the neighbourhood, even though their weapons were no match for the heavy ones used by the army.

It was an epic stand-off. After a while the revolutionaries managed to open up a road leading to the countryside. This provided me with a safe way out and I arranged to meet up with my family. At that point I hadn't seen them for a whole year. I asked my mother to come with my brothers and sisters and meet me in one of the liberated villages near Raqqa, as back then the regime still controlled the city itself. I spent two wonderful days with them. After that I kept on the

move, travelling constantly within areas controlled by the revolutionaries. I didn't get back into Raqqa until just before it was briefly liberated by rebel forces in 2013.

I've been woken up by the noise of warplanes. I can hear the sound of explosions. It's a bitter reminder of reality and the need to stop dreaming and focus on staying alive.

Outside, one of my neighbours is running round hysterically, asking if anyone has seen his son. 'He went to buy some bread.'

Those around us say that the bombs have hit my friend Ahmed's house near the Naeem roundabout. We run there as fast as we can and find scattered bodies. One of them is that of a pregnant woman. Apparently she was due to give birth in a few days' time.

The noise of the warplanes grows louder. One is overhead. We all scatter. It's white, like the ones that hit us a few days ago – a Russian plane.

After the planes have gone, I get up and walk to work. Since my father was killed, I've been working in a neighbour's shop. My boss, Abu-Muhammed, who is quietly sipping tea, gives me a weary smile. I notice he isn't smoking. This is very unusual; he usually has a cigarette with his tea. But IS has banned smoking now. After smelling his cigarette, they humiliated him outside his shop in front of everyone. Then they beat him up, as if he were a criminal.

While we are talking, two men carrying some papers go into the shop next door. Moments later, they walk into ours. They hand us both pieces of paper before leaving without a word.

The papers are an order from IS banning all televisions in shops. We have a week to remove ours. It seems it isn't enough to stop us talking to the outside world. Now we can't even look at it.

Later that day, I went to see a relative who lived a short drive across the city. I had tried to phone her first to say we were coming, but her landline wasn't working.

'It's been disconnected because I couldn't pay the bill,' she told me when I arrived. Daesh has been enforcing new charges on landlines, electricity and water.

My relative said she'd had enough and was going to try to leave the city. She planned to go to Turkey to join an uncle, and see if she could find work there. I wished her a safe journey, and hoped to God she would make it.

Back out on the street, I noticed several women walking with machine guns over their shoulders. I asked a vendor who they were.

'They're from the Khansa Brigade,' he told me.

The members of this brigade were normally wives of Daesh members, many of whom couldn't speak Arabic. Most local women hated them. They went around enforcing the Sharia dress code. While I was watching, they stopped a young woman who was standing in front of a restaurant. They demanded to know why her hands weren't covered. The woman looked close to panic and quickly apologised, saying she hadn't known that she should do this.

'Go and buy the full Islamic dress immediately!' one of the brigade women shouted. 'Otherwise you will be arrested and fined!'

The young woman nodded meekly and went on her way.

As I was finishing my sandwich, more and more Daesh fighters began filling up the café I was in. They seemed to buy whatever they pleased. It disgusted me. These men were paid hundreds of dollars a month and were given cars and accommodation, while most civilians here were getting poorer by the day and had trouble feeding their families.

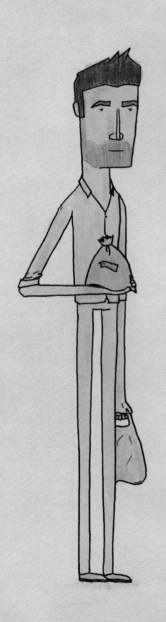

My mobile rings. It's my mother. She asks me to buy some groceries, but I can't afford much these days. Tomatoes now cost more than four hundred Syrian pounds, and rice is five hundred. It's terrible.

On the way home, I think up lots of excuses to explain why I've returned with so little food. But I don't need to. Like most parents here, my mother is just delighted that I haven't been arrested or killed and am safely back home.

I'm passing a crowd in a public square. I don't want to join them because they may be there to watch a beheading. Thank God, though, it's only a lashing this time. The offender is a member of the regime. His offence, I'm told, was carrying out a homosexual act.

A friend comes into the shop today. We haven't seen him since he was arrested by IS for the fourth time about a month ago. 'You're alive!' I shout. 'We thought you were dead.'

He laughs with a weird smile on his face. He tells me that the last time he was arrested, it was because his trousers were too long. IS insists that they should always be above ankle length. Anyone found breaking this rule has to undergo a week-long Sharia course.

As if such ridiculous charges were not bad enough, they deliberately make up some accusations, knowing them to be false. We've all witnessed this. Yet Islam does not allow convictions based on suspicions alone. Any true Muslim who has seen what Daesh does knows what fakers they are. Not only are they committing crimes against us, they are also committing crimes against our beloved religion.

That is a terrible offence, because Islam is the most precious thing we have, a glimpse of light in these very dark times.

It's morning and my mother bustles into my room warning me not to be late for Friday prayers. I spring out of bed and eat some breakfast, but I don't stop to wash up. I can't risk being beaten by IS for missing prayers just because I was doing the dishes.

On the way to my shop before prayers, I see someone I know. He walks up to me and whispers that Daesh has just thrown two teenagers to their death off a high building. He says they were accused of a homosexual act. Yet only yesterday two Daesh fighters who'd been accused of the same offence only got a lashing.

How can they say they are enforcing the word of Allah, and his justice, when they punish people for the same offence so differently?

My train of thought is cut short when one of our neighbours reminds me that it's time to pray. Like other vendors, we need to close our shop temporarily and go to the mosque. But before we set off, we see an order from Daesh telling us that we also have to attend a week-long Sharia course. This will mean shutting the shop completely for all that time. It's hard enough already trying to make a living without orders like these.

We lock the shop door and head to the mosque. When we get there, they split us up according to where we live. We all have to wait our turn. We wait and we wait, and by the time it's our turn, it's already getting dark. We're told to sit down in front of a large hairy man, who tells us that we are heretics and need to be reintroduced to Islam. He then takes my ID card and gives me a receipt with my name on it. Next to my name are the words: 'This person has repented.'

I now understand better what they are trying to do. They want to convince us that we are wrong. That they are proper Muslims and we are not. They don't trust anyone until he has attended several Sharia courses and declared that he has repented.

Abu-Muhammed and I thought we'd finished our compulsory Sharia course. But then we heard we still had to attend night classes at the mosque as well. So too did many other shop owners. This is why so many of Raqqa's shops are shut.

An old friend of mine, who had also been ordered to go to these classes, didn't show up. When an IS guy demanded to know where he was, we said he was ill. We later heard that they had raided his home. But he wasn't there.

We've now finished the week-long course and have officially re-entered Islam as born-again Muslims.

The next day, I walked to work with confident strides. A Daesh man stopped me and asked if I'd done my dawn prayers. 'Yes, of course,' I replied. But he clearly thought I was lying. 'Which part of the Quran did you read?'

I was saved from further questioning when a woman who wasn't covering her eyes properly walked past. The man rushed over to confront her. I carried on as quickly as possible.

But things got worse when I walked through the shop door. I was told that two men had been in asking where I was. I started to panic and my hands began to shake. I asked who they were. 'I don't know, but one of them was carrying a gun,' replied my boss.

Was I going to be lashed, or sent to fight for Daesh on the front line? My first thought was to run away, but I knew that they'd soon come after me.

I spent the whole day thinking about those two men and what might happen. But nobody came to get me, and as soon as the shop closed, I went straight home.

'What's wrong with you?' my mother asked. 'Why do you look so pale?' Mothers spot these sorts of things.

I had no appetite for dinner. I kept thinking how my mother would react if Daesh came to our house to get me. She kept asking me what was upsetting me, but I wouldn't say. I didn't want to worry her.

I didn't sleep all night. I don't think my mother did either. In the morning I left early and headed to the shop to open up. I'd rather they took me away there than in front of my mum.

Today has been a really scary day.

*

My friend has been sentenced to death for missing the Sharia class. Thankfully someone managed to warn him and he was able to run away before Daesh got him.

This evening I go to visit Abu-Quassim, who is nearer my father's age than mine. We sit in his children's bedroom. He says he brings close friends and other guests to this room because it has a window that overlooks the street, which can be opened to let out cigarette smoke. I ask him if all this smoke isn't bad for his children. 'They're used to it by now,' he tells me, adding that the only thing that really worries them is when he gets arrested, which has happened three times.

I can't help asking him where he gets his cigarettes from, because Daesh has banned them. He slowly shakes his head and tells me that he's always smoked and it will take more than Daesh to stop him now. I apologise for asking him so many questions. All I really want to know, I tell him, is whether he can help me deal with the desperate situation we're all in. Having lived through many troubles in the past, does he have any advice?

He begins by telling me that people here used to say that walls have ears, but they later found out that walls are deaf. The ears we fear belong to people among us, 'but they are just weak souls', he says.

He tells me, 'Live your life without considering the present. Imagine you're walking on a rope between two mountains. The present is the ground below. Walk straight ahead and focus only on crossing to the other mountain. Never look down.'

From now on, I will take his advice and try to keep walking straight ahead until I reach the other mountain. When I get there, the present will be gone.

The sun is out for the first time in days. The brighter weather makes me feel optimistic. I'm able to push away the gloomy thoughts I've had for weeks.

But the household goods in our grocery shop are getting dusty. They're just not selling. The cost of getting them here through countless regime and Daesh checkpoints has made them so expensive. We sell less in two months under Daesh than we did in a week before. And that's not just because of the soaring prices; many people just don't go out on the streets any more.

To make matters worse, Daesh recently ordered all shopkeepers to limit their mark-up on goods to 25 per cent. And they charge us tax on top of that. Then there's the cost of cleaning and electricity – when we can get it. We're basically making a loss. Traders are giving up.

The mother of a friend comes into the shop and tells me that they've arrested her son in a raid on her home. Anas was with us from the start of the revolution in 2011, but he gave up all activism when Daesh took over, getting married and settling down.

Poor guy. He didn't realise that they'd still come after him. Daesh knew of his previous involvement with the revolution and they had arrested him several times.

I try to calm his mother down, saying they're probably only questioning him, like they've done plenty of times before. But she takes no comfort from this and tells me to leave the city before they come for me too.

Her words have really got to me. I walk around the city with a broken soul, looking at all the other broken souls passing by. Each pair of eyes that passes tells a different story, a different struggle.

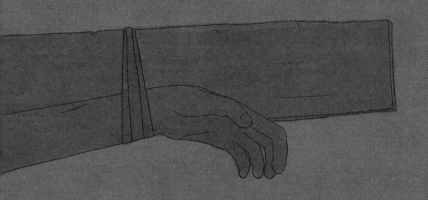

Around noon, I'm arranging the shelves when an old friend comes in to see me. He looks shocked and advises me not to take my usual route home. He says there's something he doesn't want me to see but doesn't say what.

In the end, curiosity gets the better of me.

In front of my friend's house, I see a man with his head cut off. He's been crucified too. A sign above his head reads: 'A spy, a collaborator who worked against the Islamic State.' It's Anas. I can't believe it.

I'm in such a state, I can't go home. I don't want my mother to see me like this. How could they do that? Leave his butchered body in front of his mother's house? In front of his family?

It's getting worse by the day. They're carrying out raids on the houses of anyone who ever had anything to do with the revolution. Even if it was many months or years ago. I was one of those guys. I've distanced myself from people I used to go to protests with. I don't want Daesh suspecting me or them.

✳

Today Alaa walked past the shop without coming in. He looked worried. I've known him a long time though we weren't very close until Daesh entered our city. But there aren't many people left of our age in Raqqa, and although we rarely get together in public due to fear of being noticed, we've become friends. I ran out of the shop to ask what was wrong.

Alaa told me that his mother had passed out but staff at the hospital had refused to take her in, saying there wasn't room for civilians. Priority goes to Daesh fighters. The hospital is full of them. Many have been injured in air strikes or on battlefields.

I told him that the wife of the owner of the shop next to us was a nurse and that we could ask him to call her. By the time we got to my friend's house, the nurse was already there. Alaa's mother was just suffering from shock, she said, and would be fine after she'd rested.

Then Alaa told me the full story. His mother and their neighbour Um-Waleed used to get together in the morning to have a cup of coffee before Um-Waleed went to work. Um-Waleed's son, Waleed, is a complicated guy with mental problems. I know him. He's a bit of a loner who struggled to make friends, and most of us tried to avoid him.

Waleed had joined Daesh and became committed to taking his revenge on everyone. He told Daesh that his mother had a grudge against them and promised to carry out the punishment himself. He executed his own mother in public.

Some things that Daesh are doing have come as no surprise. But many others have been much worse than what I had ever expected.

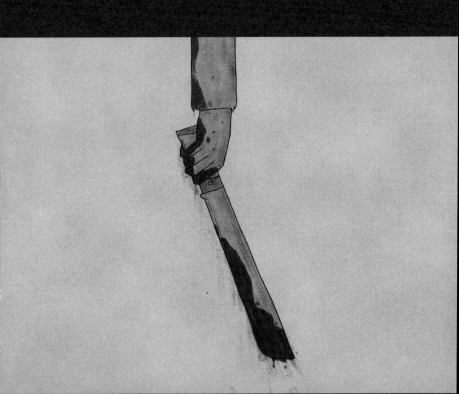

Abu-Quassim advised me to try and ignore everything that is going on around me. But however hard I try, I can't help remembering the things that have happened. When Daesh first raped my city, snatching it away from the revolutionaries who had sacrificed everything to liberate it, I became really angry. I could not accept the situation and became determined to uncover the crimes against our people. I had to tell the outside world what was happening to Raqqa.

Daesh always hurry to the location of an air strike as soon as it happens to stop us civilians going near it. Not because they fear for our safety but to prevent any media activists from taking photographs and sharing them with the outside world. After all, this would be proof of the awful situation we live in. It's very similar to the way the regime behaved. Living through the tyranny of the regime taught me some vital lessons that have been useful during life under Daesh, but these new tyrants rule with an even tighter grip.

I have got together with some young guys I met during the first popular protests against the regime. These activists have stayed in the city since Daesh took over. We all agree that something has to be done and that we should shoulder the responsibility to make it happen.

Riyad has assigned roles to each of us. My role is uploading social media messages and blogs we've written and getting them out of Raqqa. I go to an internet café and upload what we have stored on my mobile. The cafés are always full of Daesh's security guys and they execute media activists, so we have to be very careful. My material is sent to an intermediary, who passes it to my friend Mokhles on the outside. He is then able to publish it online.

We want the outside world to know what is happening. Things they might not otherwise imagine, like the executions and stonings, and casualties from air strikes. We want to tell those who have fled Raqqa how our city is coping. We also worry about those who are now refugees in unknown countries. They must be equally worried about what is happening here.

*

My friend Khalid is very kind, known for his good manners.
He was a founder member of our activist group and has
memorised the Quran in its entirety. Educated people
like him scare Daesh the most. He believes that our most
important role is to expose the true nature of Daesh,
particularly the way they use religion to cover up their
criminality, only fooling those who do not know Islam
properly. The people who fall for their lies are trying to find
a purpose in life. Khalid wants us to uncover the truth, to
stop more people joining Daesh and hopefully persuade
those who have joined to leave. He hates the way Daesh are
corrupting our religion, polluting everything our fathers and
grandfathers taught us and telling us that we are wrong
and they are right.

I see Khalid after Friday prayers. The guys all gather around
him asking for his opinion on the preacher. Though the
quotes from the Quran and Hadith[7] he used were correct,
the feeling is that they were being used to market and
promote Daesh. Khalid is becoming very impatient with
what is happening. His criticism of Daesh is getting louder.
It worries me. I try to calm him down, fearing for his safety.

Riyad sends for me to discuss Khalid. People are watching
him, asking questions about him, posing as anti-Daesh
sympathisers. He tells me that Khalid is a 'marked card' and
that we have to stay away from him. I take Riyad's words
seriously and send a message via my mother to try to warn
Khalid of the danger he is in.

7   The sayings of the Prophet.

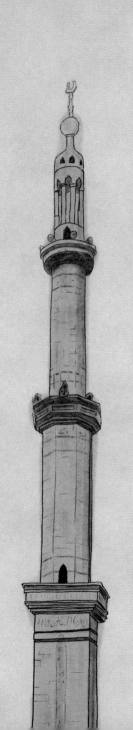

It's too late. A group of men have already broken into his house and arrested him. Soon after this he is executed for being 'an enemy of Islam and Allah'.

I will never forget this day. Daesh gathered people around them in the public square before delivering their little speech. I couldn't believe what I was seeing, nor what I was hearing. They crucified him not far from his family's home.

I have been greatly affected by Khalid's death. I am now more determined than ever to fight this criminal group and expose what they are doing. I want it to be known what they are doing to us. Not only how their actions affect us physically, but what they have done to our dreams, our revolution, our way of life. Yet I also find myself overwhelmed by fear. It's not just the horror of what happened to Khalid; it's the knowledge that the same thing might happen to me, in front of my mother.

These executions and other bloody punishments cast a long shadow of sadness across this city and the countryside beyond. There is little normal life here now. The streets are almost deserted. Most of the shops have closed because even those who brave the streets do not have money to buy anything.

The city, as well as its people, is dying at the hands of Daesh. Its spirit is being slowly strangled.

✳

My courage and determination seem to have suddenly deserted me. I have to admit that I have even tried to leave my activist group several times. I just want to be free of the constant worry. I desperately want my peace of mind back, or at least a taste of it.

I don't trust people any more, but I haven't told anyone. Perhaps they don't notice the change in me. I've always been quiet; some of my friends have gone as far as describing me as 'mysterious'. I decide to split from Riyad's group. Daesh is hunting down activists more than ever, so I do my best to avoid others like me. I will carry on doing what I'm doing, but on my own from now on.

I have been noting what is happening in my city in the form of diaries. This is a dangerous thing to do. Daesh has the city completely under their control and I am never far from them when I am writing.

The state of the shop isn't good. We haven't had a customer in days.

Today I saw a child, around eight years old, being given a weapon to execute an old man who had been accused of working with the regime. The guy was a retired army officer. Everyone was shocked. He was well known and respected. He was executed alongside a younger guy who had defected from the military. Both were slaughtered after being convicted of the same false charge – working with the regime.

Last night my activist friend Riyad, took centre stage in my dreams. First he's beheaded and crucified by Daesh, but then he rises again, more defiant than ever.

A crowd is gathering, shouting at the top of their voices, 'Riyad is leading us! Riyad, our dear friend, you're back from the dead! You are risen again after being executed by Daesh.' Riyad responds with chants against Daesh. We all repeat his words and shout, 'We are with you all the way, Riyad! Down with Daesh! Down with Daesh!'

The sound of freedom reverberates around us. And as we advance on Daesh, their fighters run for their lives.

'Samer, get up, my son, you'll be late for work.'

It is my mother. Oh God, I think, it's ten o'clock! I have to open up the shop. Abu-Muhammed said he can't come in today.

I jump out of bed and head straight to the shop, with images of last night's dream still playing in my head. It gives me a big boost. A boost I need so much in the midst of all that's been happening here.

Just after I open the shop, my friend Malek walks in behind me. He seems to have bad news.

'Samer,' he says, 'there is someone who needs to speak to you. Come to my house this evening.'

Malek's request worries me. What is this about? I feel a bit paranoid, but try to think of something else for the rest of the day. This is something I am doing a lot at the moment. Always trying to distract myself from thinking of what is happening around me.

I feel overwhelmed by hopelessness. I just can't see any light at the end of all this darkness. I know I have to fight this awful despair I'm in, but I find it hard to care about anything.

Mother tells me she wants to talk to me but then struggles to say anything. I ask her to please tell me what is on her mind, to stop torturing herself. Her words shake me to the core. 'Son,' she says, 'we have God to watch over us, so don't worry about your family.' She tells me that she knows that the situation has become unbearable, and that she is worried every minute. That she waits all day for me to come home but the anxiety doesn't stop even when I'm back. 'I worry that at any moment they will come and take you from me.' These words are bad enough, but what really gets me are the unspoken ones in her eyes. They seem to be yelling, 'Get out while you can, go before it's too late!' But leaving Raqqa, the city I love, is a big step to take.

✳

It is in my nature to be affected deeply by what is happening around me, and I spend the whole day gazing and thinking. My mind drifts in and out of dark, depressing thoughts to others that have moments of hope. Perhaps God has not completely abandoned me and may yet rid me of my worries.

I had hoped that things might change, that Daesh might suddenly disappear from our dear city. This continuing hope, however vague, makes me want to stay and hang on to all I know. In my most optimistic moments I can even smell the air of freedom.

But life has carried on getting worse rather than better. The more territory Daesh loses outside the city, the more complicated and tense things become for us here. Their fighters' behaviour grows more unpredictable every day.

✳

It's a nice sunny day. For the first time in ages there are no threatening sounds of planes in the air, something we have become wearily accustomed to. This cheers me up after many days of haunting depression.

I hear a man shouting at me, but I walk faster and don't look round, trying to ignore him. I know it's Massoud, the clerk from our local grocery shop. He's pretty infamous. He disappeared for a while and people said that he'd joined Daesh and had gone on a training course with them.

I walk faster and faster but Massoud doesn't give up. He starts calling my name in an ever louder voice, which attracts too much attention. In a bid to lose him, I take a quick left down a small side alley, which eventually leads to the shop where I work.

When I get there, I'm surprised to find that it's not open yet. This is very strange. Abu-Muhammed is never late.

Now I'm worrying again about what Massoud wanted with me. I can't take any more of this. I open up the shop and try to make myself busy.

Abu-Muhammed doesn't show up all day. After closing the shop, I go to his house to find out what has happened. His son opens the door, and as I go in, I see that Abu-Muhammed has various relatives with him. He asks me to sit down and tells me what is going on.

His twelve-year-old nephew, Mahmoud, had been missing for ten days. Earlier, Massoud, the guy who was chasing after me this morning, turned up at his brother's house and told him that Mahmoud had been killed north of Aleppo whilst fighting for Daesh. He had been brainwashed by Daesh and had run away from home after they'd fed him their nonsense about jihad, which has nothing to do with us. 'God,' says Abu-Muhammed, 'will punish them for this.'

Shocked and saddened though I am, what I hear does not surprise me. For some time now Daesh have been sending children to the front line. It shows how desperate they have become. They are using up all their cards to keep themselves going. They always say, 'We are applying the Sharia of Allah.' But it's a Sharia law they have invented themselves.

The next day, I'm at work when the sound of planes becomes deafening. As usual, the Daesh fighters in the street begin panicking and running around like headless chickens. Every time they feel threatened, they lash out at us, rather than at their actual enemies flying above us.

That night, they enforce a curfew across the city, which means I won't be able to go to Malek's house as we had planned. I call him but he refuses to discuss over the phone whatever it was he wanted to talk to me about. He says Daesh are monitoring phone calls.

I'm starving, but my mother tells me there's no bread. I make tea, using some old textbooks as fuel to boil the water. We have had no gas to cook with for months, despite Daesh controlling most of the oilfields. Instead of selling it to us, they export most of it to Iraq. They also sell to Assad's regime, even though they're supposed to be fighting them. It seems a very cosy business relationship.

Sugar is really expensive here these days, so I don't have any in my tea.

There's an old local saying: 'The hungry will still be hungry, even if they eat constantly for forty years.' Daesh aren't capable of providing even the most basic things for us. All they do is steal the little we have. We're the ones who are paying for them.

Another old saying is that bad things tend to come in clusters. How true this is. We're being told to provide money to have the roads in our city cleaned. The money they are demanding is the equivalent to a whole month's takings in the shop! They are always taking our money and adding taxes to everything. They squeeze out of us just about all we have and they keep inventing new ways to fleece us. Even the poor

in this city aren't spared. It's as if Daesh's goal is to find
the most effective way to ruin our community before they
finally leave.

✳

The next evening, I manage to get to Malek's house. Inside
there are two young men with mobile phones. I recognise
one of them. He was a regular at the anti-regime protests.
I still don't know why Malek was so insistent that I come.
As I sit down, he goes out and gets his own phone. He tells
me that he's managed to get it connected to the internet. It's
a secure connection, so Daesh won't be able to trace it.

Daesh insist that using mobile phones is a sin against
God and an unforgivable crime.

What follows is a massive surprise. Malek passes me the
phone and I hear Mokhles' voice. He was one of the first
revolutionaries and a very close friend. I haven't spoken to
him for ages. I managed it before by going to an internet
café, but since these have become so heavily monitored by
Daesh, no one uses them. He managed to escape some time
ago and is living in a rural area in northern Aleppo.

He does his best to tell me all he knows about how fellow
Syrians are coping, separated by the twin evils of the regime
and Daesh. The Syrian Democratic Forces are the ones closest
to Raqqa at the moment, but his views on them are worrying.
Even though he's experienced life under Daesh, he is very
critical of the SDF. They executed his brother, and his mother
died of a heart attack when she was told.

Amazingly, he says he would rather live in Raqqa under
Daesh's control than under the militia of the SDF. He warns
that if they enter the city we will simply be passing from one
terrible occupation to another.

This is very disappointing. I was hoping that they would liberate Raqqa and that life would become better. But I have no reason to doubt what Mokhles is telling me.

That night I go to bed with Mokhles' words in my ears. I try to read between the lines of what he told me, looking for any glimpses of hope. Any sign that things might get better soon.

✳

It's Friday, which means I have to attend prayers. Anyone who doesn't is brutally punished. Barely anyone is on the streets; everyone is already inside. There's a Daesh police car driving round and round. It reminds me of the way the regime used to circle the mosque during Friday prayers to try and stop protests breaking out when they ended.

Mokhles had asked me to take some photos of the city because he misses it and wants to see how it looks. Thank God I am not seen by Daesh. God knows what would happen if I was spotted.

That evening, I speak with Mokhles again as planned. He tells me that another friend of mine, Hassan, says hello. We talk about many things, but the state of life in our beloved city forms the bulk of our conversation.

Mokhles stands by his suspicion of the Syrian Democratic Forces. I learn that the Kurds, who form the majority of the SDF, want to form a 'federation of northern Syria'. Now it seems to me that their ambitions are clear. I find it really telling how Daesh responds to territorial advances by their enemies. For example, when the regime took Tadmur from them, it was more of a handover than a takeover. Daesh had already pulled out and moved its entire forces to Raqqa and other areas still under its control. It seems to me that there's some sort of special understanding between the regime and Daesh, like that between father and son.

I plan to go to Malek's every evening. It's really good to speak to friends and activists outside Raqqa. This longed-for communication makes the city feel a little less like a prison.

✳

I'm beginning to feel that time is running out for me in Raqqa, the city I love. Every day the expression on my mother's face grows more and more tense. That look in her eyes is telling me to get out while I still can.

I speak to Abu-Muhammed. I know he cares about me deeply and wants the best for my future. He tells me that there are some facts we have to face. That running a shop in these terrible times is getting harder and harder and that sales over the last year haven't covered our costs. He tells me that I am a young man and that it would be wrong for me to waste more of my life here. 'Son, the only thing we have now is God's mercy. That is our only hope.'

He puts a hand on my shoulder and tells me that he knows I worry about my family, but that if I want the best for them, I should leave. 'Even if your life doesn't mean much to you, it does mean a lot to others.'

His words, combined with my deep state of depression about what is happening all around me, are tipping the balance. It will be very hard for me to abandon this city. I have no idea if I will be able to bear being separated from my home and everyone I love, but maybe it really is time to leave.

I'll start thinking about where I could escape to. It will have to be one of the liberated areas. Perhaps those controlled by the Kurds and the Syrian Democratic Forces? No, that's not an option. They wrongly believe that all those living under Daesh are loyal to them.

*

Today I had the feeling that I was being followed, both on my walk to work and on my way home. It was just an instinct, but I'm convinced I'm right. I've had this experience many times in the years since I joined the revolution, and I've learned never to ignore these feelings.

I take extra care wherever I go, every step of the way. I only visit places I need to go, like the shop. Though I doubt I'll be going there much longer. Abu-Muhammed is deep in debt and I expect he'll have to close the business soon. I've already stopped working there regularly and am pretty much unemployed now. I'm struggling to imagine how I'll pay for any of the things I will need in order to escape. Nevertheless, I carry on making plans.

With extreme care I've been doing my best to stay in touch with activist friends on the outside. I tell them what's happening in this prison we now live in, hoping that they will pass this on to the world outside.

It is a rainy evening. I look around me suspiciously. The road is nearly empty. I walk quickly to Malek's house. I speak on a secure phone line he's set up to my old friend Mokhles. Mokhles sounds worried. He tells me he's been told by an intelligence cell he's in touch with that I've been blacklisted by Daesh and need to get out of Raqqa as soon as possible. He goes on to explain how he and others managed to escape. I first need to find a smuggler to take me to Al-Bab city, and then another to guide me to a liberated area controlled by the Free Syrian Army. He warns me that I'll need to be careful every step of the way.

Malek tells me that Abu-Saleh, a local cab driver, has been helping people escape.

Later that night, I go and see Abu-Saleh and explain that I want his help to get out of the city. Listening to my story, he says he's surprised I haven't left already. He tells me it will cost $200, possibly less if I can persuade other people to travel with me and pay some of the fare. For now, he says, I should keep my head down and wait to hear from him.

In normal times I'm not good at waiting. Now, filled with stress and worry, I'm worse than ever. I pace up and down, up and down. Now that Mokhles has confirmed that Daesh are looking for me, I expect to be arrested at any moment.

It's hard to look at my mother. I know I may never see her again. I find it difficult to think clearly any more. It's impossible to put my feelings into words.

Two nights go by. I'm very cautious. I'm very scared. I sleep in the arms of my mother like a little child.

Late at night there is a knock on the door. I approach nervously. I hear Malek's voice telling me to open it.

'Samer,' he says, 'here is some money to help out. It's not much but it comes with love from your friends. Remember, we are all one now.' He tells me that he has negotiated with the smuggler on my behalf and paid him. The money he is giving me now is for my family, to help them after I've gone. The driver will be leaving just before dawn. I've been told to take only essential things with me; that I must leave my mobile phone as well as anything else with names or numbers stored in it. There are lots of Daesh checkpoints and they search everyone.

Malek promises to be the link between me and my family once I've escaped. I thank him, and he bids me farewell. 'God be with you, my brother Samer.'

I don't know how I'm going to say my goodbyes to my family, but when I turn around, I see my mother standing there. She was listening to my conversation with Malek. She is crying but trying to comfort me. She insists we won't be parted for long. 'Look after yourself,' she pleads. 'Lead a decent life, always be honourable.'

She's speaking as if she thinks we may never see each other again.

I get ready to leave in a hurry. I don't need long to pack because I can hardly take anything with me. If I was seen carrying big bags at this time of the morning, it would be obvious I was leaving. I can't risk that.

As I open the front door, Abu-Saleh's old minibus draws up. 'Goodbye, Mother,' I whisper. 'Goodbye, my brothers and sisters. Look after yourselves.'

Abu-Saleh tells me that we need to pick up the rest of the passengers before the sun rises, otherwise it will be impossible to make it through the checkpoints. He tells me that he does this journey every week and nobody has been arrested yet. Except, he adds, one person who was so scared when they were stopped by a Daesh patrol that he ended up saying all the wrong things. He tells me that we need to be calm. All we should say if we are stopped is that we're going to another area under Daesh control to buy some goods.

We pick up a pregnant woman with two children, a man in his thirties and another man who looks familiar. He is extremely nervous and doesn't say much.

It doesn't take long to leave the administrative borders of Raqqa city behind. Abu-Saleh knows the route by heart and we manage to avoid a string of Daesh checkpoints.

As we are passing through a small village, a man on a tractor stops us. He tells Abu-Saleh that there's a newly erected checkpoint ahead and suggests we take another route. Our driver thanks him and darts down a small side road, but this diversion doesn't turn out well. The road has been damaged by an air strike and we can't get through. He turns around and we head back to the village. He takes

us to a relative of his who lives there. While we're eating breakfast, he drives off to do some reconnaissance.

Two hours later, he is back. He's been told by a friend that our best way through to the liberated areas is via a small village near Al-Ra'ee, so we'll head there instead of going to Al-Bab city. We don't need to travel as far as we'd anticipated because rebel forces have recently advanced and taken back some territory from Daesh. But we'll still have to take a string of diversions for the next hundred miles. After that, we'll need to get out and walk through the night.

As we're passing through Manbij, a town about ninety miles from Raqqa, we hear the sound of planes overhead.

Our driver screeches to a halt and tells us to get out and take cover. He's worried that our vehicle might prove an attractive target.

Soon we're back on the road. The places we pass through are almost empty. They look like ghost villages. There probably are lots of ghosts given the death toll in this area over recent years. Somehow, when we finally arrive at our next stop, we manage to find someone to host us.

*

Normally we would have covered the short distance we have travelled in a few hours, but it has taken us two whole days to reach Al-Ra'ee. But Abu-Saleh reminds us that it is better to be safe than sorry.

His part is now done. He hands us over to another smuggler, whose job it is to get us to the liberated areas. This last leg is clearly going to take time. He shows us to a house where we are told to rest up and wait for him to return. On no account, he insists, are we to leave. Apparently Daesh are especially active at the moment because the Free Syrian Army has been advancing across this area.

In the house, I begin talking to my fellow passengers. The guy I'd thought was in his thirties is called Ali. He's from Deir Ezzor, and after graduating, he got a good job working for a petroleum company. But Daesh took over the oilfield and tried to force him to join, so he fled.

I've finally realised why I recognised the other man, who has barely spoken. He's in his forties and was a member of the local council in Raqqa when the revolutionaries took over from the regime. I know that he was arrested by Daesh a number of times, so I can well understand why he had to get out.

The pregnant woman tells me that her husband was a fighter with the Free Syrian Army but had recently left to help her look after their children. One night Daesh came to their home and took him away. He was executed, convicted of being an apostate. God knows what that actually means.

*

We thought we would be moving on later that night, but the smuggler appears and tells us the time isn't right. It looks like we are going to have to carry on waiting.

The next night he tells us that we are continuing our journey to freedom. But soon after leaving the house, we are shot at. The gunfire is coming from some distance away, but the smuggler quickly turns us around and we run back to the house. The waiting game continues.

Every day we hear that more and more people have crossed successfully into rebel-held areas. But we're also warned that many others have either been arrested or killed as they attempted to flee. We continue to wait.

I have another big issue to worry about. I don't have enough money to pay the second smuggler and can't think what to do. I end up confessing my fears to the pregnant woman. Her response makes my heart leap for joy. She offers to help me if I help her with her children.

✳

Several nights go by. Ali and the silent man manage to cross over to the nearby liberated area unharmed. I'm still here with the pregnant woman and her children. We've been joined by some other would-be escapees who are intending to use the same route.

It's now ten o'clock and we have taken the decision to try and cross tonight. I will do all I can to look after the children, which will mean carrying them when necessary. I am determined to make sure that no harm comes to either of them.

We listen to our instructions from the smuggler, who knows the route we must take. He tells us to first follow the right-hand path and then the left. In all we will have to walk for ten miles. After that, we'll be safe. But he warns us to be

extremely careful at all times. It's not just Daesh that we must watch out for; there are landmines everywhere.

We head off in groups.

'Come on, sister,' I tell the young mother. 'We have to pick up the pace a bit.' We hear a series of pops in the distance and a stream of bullets fly in our direction. They must have seen us coming from a long way away.

As panic starts to build, I see a big rock. It must be the one that the smuggler told us was a landmark on our path to safety.

It's a terrifying walk. Carrying a child under each arm, I'm too scared to look behind us. All the time I worry about stepping on a landmine. If that happens, we'll all be killed. But finally we arrive in an area controlled by the Free Syrian Army. Thank God!

Cautiously, kneeling on the ground, I scan the landscape. All of a sudden I see an armed man approaching us on a motorbike. He is some distance away and it's hard to tell which side he is on. He doesn't look like a Daesh fighter, but it's hard to be sure. I try to think of what to do, knowing that a wrong move now might cost us our lives.

We dive out of sight behind some rocks, but the younger of the two children is crying and won't stop.

I can hear the motorbike getting closer and closer. I can tell he's almost on us.

'Show your faces. Do it now. Don't be afraid. We are your brothers in the Free Syrian Army.'

Oh my God. I can't believe what I'm hearing. Just as I am trying to take this in, several shells explode in the ground nearby.

It turns out we're in a sort of no-man's-land, a border area between two different forces. The motorcyclist is shouting, 'Hurry, we must leave.'

He says he'll take the woman and children and come back for me. I ask the woman if she is prepared to go with him, but she doesn't answer. She just asks the soldier to swear to us that he really is one of the revolutionaries and not a member of Daesh. He does so quickly and then starts screaming that there's no more time for talking because the shelling is getting closer and closer.

Finally, the Free Syrian Army soldier comes back to where I'm waiting. I climb onto his bike and we bump and roar towards FSA lines. As we arrive at our destination, I feel as if I am being reborn. There before me are some old friends and fellow activists. My joy is simply indescribable.

Realising I have come from a Daesh-controlled area, so many people have questions. I know they have friends or relatives still in Raqqa and are desperate to know how they're surviving.

I am very tired and really worried for my family. My danger may be over but theirs is not. I can't stop thinking about them.

A short while later, I meet my dear friend Mokhles. Somehow we managed to stay in touch throughout the last two terrible years. 'Samer,' he yells, 'you're alive! You're free!' He's crying. I'm crying. I throw myself in his arms.

After we've calmed down a bit, we set off to an internet café. I get through to Malek. 'It's Samer,' I tell him. 'Please let my family know that I'm out and in one piece. I've made it. It's over.'

✳

Every person starts their journey of life with a dream that they live in hope of achieving one day. There are many obstacles along the way. These stop some people, while others carry on.

I'm trying to find the remnants of my dream. It's fading away in the midst of an overwhelming feeling of disappointment.

As I write these words, sitting on the dusty ground, I am surrounded by thousands of refugees. Like me they were forced to flee their homes, leaving behind broken dreams of their own.

I still have hope for my country's people. It springs from those who risk their lives to oppose injustice and oppression. But in the current circumstances, I'm not convinced that the sacrifices such people have made were really worth it.

Mokhles has taken me to a camp that is now home to a lot of people from Eastern Syria, where I am from. I meet Abu-Ahmed, who fled when Daesh started targeting him. He is very humble, which is typical of most people from our area. As we enter his tent, an embarrassed look sweeps across his face. He has little to offer us and there's barely anywhere to sit. Much of the available room is taken up by his disabled child. His wife is six months pregnant and also needs space to rest.

Abu-Ahmed tells us that his brother was seventeen when he was sentenced to death for allegedly plotting against Daesh. His family didn't know about the accusation until they heard his execution being announced over the loudspeaker. Abu-Ahmed says his brother had been naïve. He was caught in an internet café with an incriminating photo on his phone. The picture was of a friend who was martyred fighting against Daesh before they took control of Raqqa.

✳

I stuck to my city for as long as I could. It gave me some of my most beautiful memories and I wanted to stay and help in its time of need. I was willing to bear the difficult times. I was prepared to die there too.

If it weren't for my mother, I would never have left. But she was so afraid. She knew that I was in their sights and it would not have been long before they pulled the trigger. So my new life in exile has begun.

The area I am in is full of people like me. Thousands who have fled their homes, running from either Daesh or Assad's regime. Their suffering, and mine, is not over yet. It's not even close to being over.

There isn't enough food or medicine in the camp; the regime's warplanes circle above us.

Many people here tell me they wish they were already dead. Many are hoping to cross into Turkey, but the border is completely closed. It's hopeless. Many have been maimed by the regime's war machine. Some are missing limbs. These injuries have a dramatic impact on them and those who care for them. Every single person here has lived with horror. Yet instead of weeping or cursing, they all try to help each other.

✳

I carry many of my memories in a small bag. Photos of people and places. Stray, random bits of my past, which probably don't exist any more. Amongst them is a picture of an old school friend. For all I know, he may be dead now. Then there's a photo of our neighbour, who died alongside his children in an air strike. One of my old friend who was crucified by Daesh. Here, a picture of our destroyed house. Others of our street, which is now ruined and empty.

But I keep some of my dearest pictures in my head. There's the beautiful girl I spent the happiest moments of my life with, until fate tore us apart. Fellow students who studied alongside me. I have no hope of ever seeing these people again.

I try to get my mind off such things by looking around me. The present is full of problems, and by engaging with these, I help free my mind from the past. I cling to the hope that although these precious memories are gone, I may find new ones if, one day, I can return to my home. This is my hope.

✳

Some fellow activists have been helping people in one of the camps on the Syrian Turkish border. I joined them there, but didn't try to get to know anyone well. I don't want to make friends. It is a new rule I apply to my life now. Don't get too close to people, because you probably won't know them long. Events will soon pull you apart.

✳

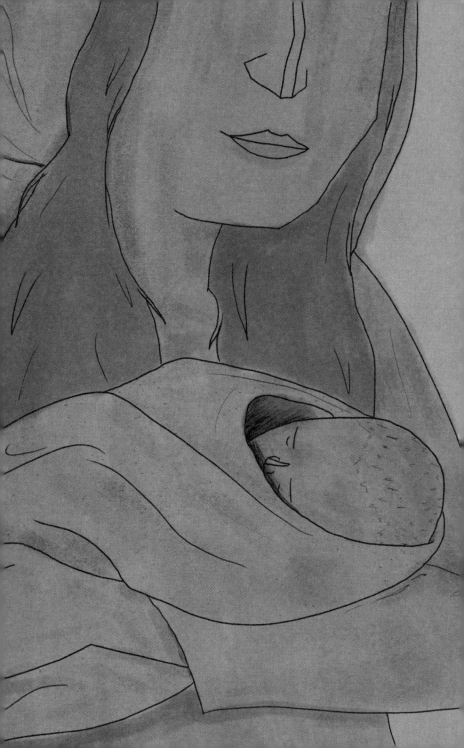

One rainy night, a woman screams. She's the widow of a Free Syrian Army fighter who was executed by Daesh. Soon afterwards, she fled to this area of Aleppo, which is controlled by FSA forces. Many camps have sprung up to accommodate people like her.

She is about to give birth, right here, out in the open. There is no hospital, no clinic, not even a single doctor. The area is completely destroyed. It is under siege from the regime's forces on one side, Kurdish militias on another, and Daesh on the third side.

Some women try to help her, but they have nothing but their hands. Thankfully, with the help of God, they succeed and the woman gives birth.

The first angry cries of her newborn baby drown out everything, even the roar of distant gunfire and air strikes.

Maybe the baby is screaming for its absent father, or just asking for a crib to lie in. Or is it pleading for an end to the constant killing and destruction and calling on God to take it back to the womb, away from this place?

You have the right to say all these things, little baby. But many who hear your cries see your arrival as a blessing. You give your family hope, and this spreads to others. I find myself thinking: maybe one day you will be our salvation, little one.

The world that you have been born into isn't that different to the one I grew up in. Although we had peace, nobody had any rights. You can still see defeat in the eyes of our fathers, and despair in those of our mothers. We may have had peace back then, but we paid a heavy price for it. Five years of revolution is not enough to get rid of a tyrannical regime that has plagued us for forty years.

The fact that the world is standing idly by, just watching what is happening, does not surprise anyone here any more. Everyone I meet, whether it is a child or an old person who has witnessed many horrors, pins their hopes on our own revolutionaries. The outside world has not answered our calls.

Some countries do worse than just stand by. They have given the regime help in killing its people. They continue to do this while thousands of families live out in the open with nothing to protect them from the rain, the sun and the bombs.

I believe that the worst crime a country can commit is to put its own self-interest before the lives of innocent people. But perhaps helping criminal groups like Assad's regime to cover their crimes is an even bigger outrage. Every informed and open-minded person knows how much our people are suffering.

We hold on to the idea that in the end, good will prevail. History will show generations to come what was right and what was wrong. Hopefully the world will learn from this and stop it happening again. As one of our oldest sayings goes: 'He who plants a good seed gets a good tree.'

All we are left with is hope. Hope that our country will rebuild itself. Hope that the sacrifices made by our people will finally banish the cruelty and evil that has long stalked our land.

For now, this is all we can do.

First American edition published in 2017 by
Interlink Books
An imprint of
Interlink Publishing Group, Inc.
46 Crosby Street, Northampton, MA 01060
www.interlinkbooks.com

Published simultaneously in Great Britain in 2017 by Hutchinson,
Random House

Library of Congress Cataloging-in-Publication Data available

978-1-56656-005-4

Typeset in Karmina Sans by Lindsay Nash
Printed and bound in Italy

MIX
Paper from
responsible sources
FSC® C018179